Asking Questions About Food Advertising

TRY OUR *Homestyle*

HAMBURGERS

100% Beef!

25¢

BEST IN T

LAURA PERDEW

Published in the United States of America by Cherry Lake Publishing
Ann Arbor, Michigan
www.cherrylakepublishing.com

Consultants: Rachel L. Bailey, Assistant Professor, The Edward R. Murrow College of Communication, Washington State University; Marla Conn, ReadAbility, Inc.
Editorial direction and book production: Red Line Editorial
Book design: Sleeping Bear Press

Photo Credits: Shutterstock Images, cover, 1, 16, 19, 21, 22, 27; Joshua Rainey/Shutterstock Images, 5; iStockphoto, 6, 14, 25; © 2015 America's Milk Companies ℠, 9; BananaStock/Thinkstock, 10; Juan Monino/iStockphoto, 13; Aleksandr Markin/Shutterstock Images, 28

Library of Congress Cataloging-in-Publication Data

Perdew, Laura.
  Asking questions about food advertising / by Laura Perdew.
    pages cm. -- (Asking questions about media)
  Includes bibliographical references and index.
  ISBN 978-1-63362-487-0 (hardcover : alk. paper) -- ISBN 978-1-63362-503-7 (pbk. : alk. paper) -- ISBN 978-1-63362-519-8 (pdf ebook) -- ISBN 978-1-63362-535-8 (hosted ebook)
  1. Advertising--Food--Juvenile literature. 2. Advertising--Juvenile literature. I. Title.

  HF6161.F616P47 2015
  659.19'664--dc23

                         2015005522

Cherry Lake Publishing would like to acknowledge the work of
the Partnership for 21st Century Skills. Please visit www.p21.org
for more information.

Printed in the United States of America
Corporate Graphics

ABOUT THE AUTHOR

Laura Perdew is an author, writing consultant, and former middle-school teacher. She writes fiction and nonfiction for children, including numerous titles for the education market. She is also the author of *Kids on the Move! Colorado*, a guide to traveling through Colorado with children. Laura lives and plays in Boulder with her husband and twin boys.

TABLE OF CONTENTS

CHAPTER 1

ADVERTISING AVALANCHE

You've been planning a movie marathon with friends for weeks. Before everyone arrives, you go to the grocery store to find the perfect snacks. You skip the produce section and head straight for the soda aisle. You debate which one to buy. There are so many choices! Finally you decide on the one that your favorite football player drinks. In the snack section you go for the chips with the advertisement that makes you laugh. For your friends who are sleeping over, you also pick up a box of cereal. The kids rapping in the commercial for the cereal always seem to be having fun.

So why did you make the choices you did? Your decision was probably influenced by advertising. A 2013 study showed that children younger than 12 are exposed to an average of 13.1 ads for food and beverages each day. Companies spend a great amount of time and money creating those advertisements. They want their product to be the one you recognize and choose over all the others. To do this, companies take great care to

The aisles of your local grocery store offer you many food choices.

These girls had many options for snacks at their sleepover.
Their choices were probably influenced by advertising.

construct messages that will connect with their target
audience.

To fully understand media messages, you must
deconstruct them. In other words, you need to take
the advertisements apart and look at them. One way to
do this is by asking questions:

- Who created and paid for the ad?
- Who is the target audience for the advertisement?
- What tools are used to grab a viewer's attention?

- Which **values** and **lifestyles** are represented? Which are omitted?

These questions will help you understand how media messages are constructed and how advertisements are intended to influence buyers like you.

SLOGANS

One way advertisers grab **consumers**' attention is with catchy **slogans**. If the phrases are catchy enough, and repeated in ads enough times, they become part of our culture. Can you match the slogans with their products? If so, the advertisers have done their jobs well.

Tostitos	The Snack that Smiles Back
Skittles	Live Mas
Taco Bell	They're Magically Delicious
Goldfish	I'm Lovin' It
Lucky Charms	Bring the Party
McDonald's	Taste the Rainbow

CHAPTER 2

Paying for Ads

When you see a food advertisement, one of the first questions to ask is who created and paid for it. This may seem like a simple question. Of course, the company that makes the product made the ad because it wants you to buy that product. Right? Not exactly. Most advertisements are created by advertising agencies hired by a company or group with a product to sell.

Let's look at the ad campaign for milk titled "Milk Life." The **text** of these ads features individuals jumping, walking, dancing, and more. The people all have milk spouting and spinning around them in the form of wings, propellers, capes, or parachutes, to simulate the power of milk. The catchphrase reads, "What 8 grams of protein look like when...." The ending of the phrase changes, depending on the activity in the ad. The **subtext**, or underlying message, in all of them is that drinking milk will empower you to do amazing things.

The ads were created by a group called Milk Processor Education Program (MilkPEP). At first it might seem that this is a group trying to educate people about milk. This is only partly true. The group *does* want people to learn about the power

Milk has 8 grams of high-quality protein. Which could be the difference between just living life...and milking it.

Start every day with the power of protein. milk life

milklife.com

Recent ads for milk sell the image that you can do amazing things if you drink milk.

Children sometimes use "pester power" to get their parents to buy the products they want.

of milk. They want people to talk about milk's nutritional benefits, especially protein. Yet MilkPEP is a coalition of milk processors across the county. They are companies that produce milk for consumption and make a profit from selling milk. They stay in business only if consumers buy their product.

TRENDS IN FOOD ADVERTISING

A 2013 study by the Yale Rudd Center for Food Policy and Obesity revealed that the average child (ages 2 to 11) is exposed to almost 5,000 food and beverage advertisements on television every year. That's 13.1 per day. Those numbers are even greater for teenagers. Further, the study indicated that the number of food and beverage commercials has risen steadily since 2007. Ads increasingly target kids because they have "pester power." Companies know that children often beg and plead—or worse—until their parents give in and buy certain products. Experts estimate that this type of "kidfluence" leads directly to hundreds of billions of dollars of food purchases by adults.

While the numbers of ads have increased, the categories of food- and beverage-related ads have remained the same. Kids see more ads for fast food than for any other category. Cereal ranked second for ads targeted toward ages 2 to 11. Advertisements for candy products, also a popular item marketed toward children, doubled between 2007 and 2013. Commercials for healthy foods such as bottled water, vegetables, and fruit represent less than 5 percent of the ads aimed at kids. Yet the number of dairy product ads has gone up by 86 percent (for children ages 2 to 11).

HITTING THE TARGET

Advertisements are constructed so that they will appeal to people based on age, gender, ethnicity, class, or interests. When you see an advertisement, ask yourself, "Who is the target audience?"

Lunchables—prepackaged lunches for kids—have been around since the 1980s. In 2012, Kraft introduced a new product, Lunchables with Smoothie. In one TV commercial, "Lunchroom Mystery," a tween boy sits in the cafeteria staring at his boring, gray metal lunchbox, wondering what's inside. Tension builds as he warily

Lunchables have become a staple of many children's diets.

unlatches the lid and opens it. He pulls out his
Lunchables package and holds it over his head while the
students around him cheer. The text at the end of the ad
promotes the fruit smoothie made with real fruit, and a
lunch packed with fun.

Who is the target audience for this ad? The obvious
answer is hungry tweens. You can tell because of the
age of all the actors in the lunchroom. They all appear to
be of late-elementary or middle-school age. But what
about gender, race, or class? The commercial includes

students of both genders, and a variety of ethnicities. The kids are wearing all kinds of clothes, from a boy with glasses and a sweater vest and girls in trendy clothes to the featured student in a hoodie. Further, the cafeteria appears to be in an older building, perhaps targeting middle-class students. The ad is designed to

Advertisements targeting children often feature attractive young models wearing trendy clothes.

CHANGING TARGETS

Kraft rolled out another new product in 2013 called Lunchables Uploaded. The new lunch includes larger portions of the foods that kids love, including a deep-dish pizza. They are packaged in silver and gray boxes, as opposed to the traditional yellow Lunchables boxes. The campaigns include the phrase, "Take it up a notch." Who is the target audience? Teenagers. The more sophisticated colors and larger portions, as well as the word "uploaded," were carefully selected to appeal to a teen market.

appeal to most tweens because it presents a variety of kids in a setting familiar to young students.

Don't forget, however, the spot at the end of the commercial about the fruit smoothie. Certainly kids interested in making healthy food choices are part of the targeted audiences. Yet the person buying the Lunchables—usually a parent—is the target for the plug about real fruit in the smoothies. The subtext of this ad implies that busy parents can feel good about the prepackaged lunch because it provides a nutritious

The popularity of McDonald's soared when it began targeting children with its advertising.

meal. However, despite this underlying message, the target audience must also consider what's not in the ad. The detailed nutritional information is missing, which is something that both parents and kids might want to know.

McDonald's Advertising Success

When Ray Kroc took over McDonald's in 1961, he knew that he had to get the word out about his restaurants. He took an innovative approach that targeted children. Kroc marketed his restaurants as places for kids: They were all-American, clean, and safe. By doing this, Kroc bet that if kids loved his commercials, they would beg to eat at McDonald's, and they would bring along their parents or grandparents.

In the early 1960s, McDonald's introduced Ronald McDonald to the public. Ads featuring the clown mascot first ran in Washington, DC. After great success, they soon aired nationwide during Saturday morning cartoons. This made the McDonald's clown a household name. Kroc didn't stop there. In order to make McDonald's even more attractive, he built small playgrounds in the restaurants. They were designed with a specific look in order to appeal to children. Later, Kroc introduced the promise of happiness for kids in boxed meals with toys called Happy Meals. The success of McDonald's advertising campaign led to a boom in ads targeting children beginning in the 1980s. Companies had previously dismissed children as their target audience, but they quickly realized children's consumer power.

CHAPTER 4

CATCHING YOUR EYE

Companies use various **marketing** techniques to persuade you to buy their products. Sometimes their ads show ordinary people in the hope that you'll identify with them and recognize shared values or needs. Other times they use an expert, hoping you will rely on the expert's authority when making food choices. Advertisers also use promotions, humor, fear, or a "warm and fuzzy" approach (think puppies and cute kids) to get your attention.

Advertisers use many different techniques—such as cute kids—to get your attention.

One of the most popular tools of persuasion is repetition. Some commercials are shown over and over. This makes those products seem familiar to you, which in turn makes you more likely to buy them. Repetition is also used within a commercial by repeating the text— the messages, images, or words associated with the product.

Branded characters are also used to sell products, especially when marketing to children. Think about Ronald McDonald, Chester Cheetah, and Cap'n Crunch.

CELEBRITY ENDORSEMENTS

Marketers often employ celebrities to endorse their products. Who wouldn't want to drink the same soda as a rock star? Or eat the same cereal as an Olympic swimmer? Celebrities get our attention and help persuade us to buy certain items. Pop star Beyoncé does ads for Pepsi, while Pepsi's rival, Coca-Cola, uses Taylor Swift to endorse Diet Coke. Lunchables Uploaded has an ad starring skateboarder Rob Dyrdek.

Other companies use movie or cartoon characters to sell their products. All these characters appeal to children and thus promote a brand name.

Another reason you might be persuaded to buy a certain food or drink item is because everyone else is doing it. That technique is called the **bandwagon** approach. Marketers create subtext in the ads suggesting that everyone in a certain peer group is eating or drinking a product. The ad appeals to people's desire to be included. No one wants to be left out! Any ad that boasts "millions served" or "join the millions" is trying to get you to jump on board, too.

Similarly, many ads use **association**. They attempt to link something desirable with a product. These messages depict people having fun, being popular, and looking great while also enjoying a certain food. The implied subtext is that if you eat the same thing, you will experience the same positive results. For example, a Reese's Puffs cereal ad features a teen and his little brother sharing an "epic" breakfast together. Mornings can be this fun in your house, too, if you eat Reese's Puffs!

Chester Cheetah is one of many branded characters used by food companies to appeal to children.

Pop star Beyoncé is one of many celebrities whom food and beverage companies use to advertise their products.

Another trend in food marketing is called stealth advertising. This is a way for companies to increase brand awareness without you noticing the advertisement. Product placement is one of the best examples of this. Have you ever seen a show where the actors or hosts are drinking Coke? Or a movie where a certain candy is eaten? In the movie *E.T. the Extra-Terrestrial*, the characters ate Reese's Pieces, a relatively unknown candy at the time. When the movie was released in 1982, sales of Reese's Pieces increased 66 percent. Other companies have created online interactive features or games that are actually advertisements for their products. Likewise, many websites include logos from other companies on their pages.

BRAND STICKINESS

Advertisers want their brands to stick in your mind. They have used scientific studies to determine the best way to make people remember their product. One of the best ways for marketers to create "brand stickiness" is to use repetition. Studies also have found that running the same ad multiple times is more effective at getting viewers to recognize a brand than running a variety of ads for the same product.

CHAPTER 5

WHAT'S THE MESSAGE?

All media messages represent certain values and lifestyles. The key is to critically assess which values and lifestyles are exhibited, which are omitted, and why.

For example, Green Giant has an ad that shows a 10-year-old boy eating dinner (including his vegetables!) with his family. Later, he wins a game of basketball outside with his father. At the end, the ad claims, "It's easy to eat like a giant, and feel like a green giant." The values of family, health, and eating together are conveyed in the main text. The lifestyle represented in the ad is one of a healthy, Caucasian, middle-class family, with a mom, a dad, and two kids.

Values and lifestyles are also apparent in an ad's subtext. The advertisement's underlying positive messages include the importance of healthy eating and

Many food advertisements imply that their products are an important part of family meals.

of eating together as a family. A fun after-dinner activity is also a positive message, as is showing a parent and child involved in the activity together. However, the unintended negative message is that basketball is just for the guys. The mother and the sister are not involved

Marketing Food to Kids

Childhood obesity is a major concern in the United States. Many say excessive advertisements for sugary and high-fat junk foods targeted at children, and the lack of ads for healthy foods, contribute to the problem. Companies spend billions of dollars on these ads each year, hoping to boost sales and create brand loyalty. A government board regulates advertising aimed at children, but the media also tells advertisers what it will or won't allow. In 2012, Disney announced that it would no longer run junk food ads on its channels beginning in 2015. Further, all food advertisements must meet Disney's strict nutritional guidelines. Any item with too much salt, fat, or sugar per serving is not allowed on the Disney channels.

When you see an advertisement, ask yourself who is in the ad and who is missing. That can help you understand who is the target of the ad.

in the basketball game. In this case, one also might wonder who cleaned up the dishes.

Which lifestyles and values are left out of the ad? People of color, older people, poor families, single adults, gay parents, and other types of nontraditional families are all left out of this ad. Does that mean that Green Giant doesn't want to sell its products to those people? Not necessarily. Advertising works best when it reaches the audience reflected in the ad. The Green Giant ad in question would be most effective if aired during a show with an audience similar to the people represented in that ad. To reach a nontraditional family, the advertiser might run a different ad during a different show.

We all face a number of tough choices when it comes to the food we eat.

Rhythm of Life

Another advertisement appeared on TV in 2015 called "Rhythm of Life." The ad for Campbell's Soups features people of a variety of ethnicities, genders, and ages. They are engaged in various activities from marching band to fly fishing to tap dancing. The activities take place in many different indoor and outdoor settings. The values represented in the ad include fitness, having fun, and healthy eating. The ad gives the sense that everyone, regardless of age, race, and class, should have such fun— and eat Campbell's Soup afterward.

Advertising is a big part of the budget for major food and beverage companies. You come across many ads for those products every day. When you see them, keep in mind what the ads' creators are doing to get you to buy their products. An informed approach can help you make better purchasing decisions for yourself and your friends.

THINK ABOUT IT

When you see a food or beverage ad, think about who created and paid for it. What do they have to gain by running the ad?

Who do you think is the target audience for the advertisement?

What tools does the ad use to grab your attention?

What values and lifestyles are represented and omitted in the ad? What does that tell you about who they're trying to reach?

LEARN MORE

FURTHER READING

Haugen, David M. *How Does Advertising Impact Teen Behavior?* Detroit, MI: Greenhaven Press, 2008.

Hicks, Aubrey. *Does Advertising Tell the Truth?* New York: Cavendish Square Publishing, 2014.

Lusted, Marcia Amidon. *Advertising to Children*. Minneapolis, MN: Abdo Publishing, 2009.

WEB LINKS

Advertising Age
www.adage.com
This online magazine has up-to-date information on trends and news in advertising.

iSpot.tv
www.ispot.tv/browse
A great resource for browsing recent television commercials.

Media Literacy Project Deconstruction Gallery
www.medialiteracyproject.org/deconstructions
Founded in 1993, this organization seeks to create critical, well-informed media consumers. This gallery has great examples of numerous deconstructed advertisements.

GLOSSARY

association (us-soh-see-AY-shuhn) an advertising tool which links a product with something positive, like fun, happiness, or popularity

bandwagon (BAND-wag-uhn) an advertising tool that shows lots of people buying and enjoying a product, thus implying that everyone else is doing it, so you should, too

consumers (kuhn-SOO-murz) those who purchase products or services

deconstruct (dee-kuhn-STRUHKT) to take apart an advertisement in order to critically understand its message

lifestyles (LIFE-stilez) the ways in which people live

marketing (MAR-kit-ing) the act of promoting and selling products

slogans (SLOH-guhnz) catchy phrases used in advertising a product

subtext (SUHB-tekst) the hidden or underlying messages in an advertisement

text (tekst) the actual words, images, and/or sounds in an advertisement

values (VAL-yoos) a person's principles or standards of behavior; one's judgment of what is important in life

INDEX